Amazing Questions & Answers

Dinosaurs

Om KIDZ
An imprint of Om Books International

Om Kidz | Om Books International

Reprinted in 2024

Corporate & Editorial Office
A-12, Sector 64, Noida 201 301
Uttar Pradesh, India
Phone: +91 120 477 4100
Email: editorial@ombooks.com
Website: www.ombooksinternational.com

Sales Office
107, Ansari Road, Darya Ganj
New Delhi 110 002, India
Phone: +91 11 4000 9000
Email: sales@ombooks.com
Website: www.ombooks.com

ISBN: 978-93-52763-01-6

Printed in India

10 9 8 7 6 5 4

What did
dinosaurs eat?
What?
When?
How did
dinosaurs fly?
When did Theropods
live on Earth?
How?
Why?
Why did dinosaurs have tails?

CONTENTS

What?

What is a dinosaur?

Dinosaurs were one of the several kinds of reptiles that lived millions of years ago. Different kinds of dinosaurs lived on Earth at different points of time; some were herbivorous while others were carnivorous animals. Many of them were huge and fierce, while some were small and shy. Dinosaurs are not found today as they became extinct a long time ago.

Pocket fact

Was it a dragon?
It is believed that the first possible dinosaur fossils (some teeth) were discovered 3,500 years ago in China. At that time, people did not know about dinosaurs, so they thought that the teeth belonged to a dragon.

Try this

Which of the following is not a dinosaur? Mosasaurs, Ichthyosaurs, Pterosaurs, Stegosaurus and Dimetrodon.

What was the world like when dinosaurs ruled the Earth?

It was much different from what it is today! Dinosaurs lived around 230 million years ago. At that time, the world was a much hotter place than it is today. Plants such as mosses, ferns and evergreen trees grew at that time. Birds, mammals and humans also didn't exist in that period. However, there were some lizard-like reptiles.

Their colour remains unknown!
Since no real dinosaur skin remains today, we don't know what colour the dinosaurs were. Palaeontologists state that dinosaur skin was probably drab-green shades of gray in colour, allowing them to blend in with their surrounding environments. Since modern-day animals like elephants and rhinoceroses, tend to be dully coloured, many palaeontologists think that dinosaurs had similar skin colour, too.

Try this!

Draw three of your favourite dinosaurs and paint them with colours of your choice.

Pocket fact

We didn't eat fruits!
Herbivorous dinosaurs ate plants called ferns, conifers and cycads. They didn't eat fruits or berries because till then fruit-bearing plants hadn't appeared on the Earth!

What did dinosaurs eat?

Some ate plants while others ate animals! Most of the dinosaurs were herbivores, or animals that ate plants. These include Stegosaurus, Brachiosaurus and other members of the Sauropod family. The carnivorous dinosaurs ate small animals, including other dinosaurs. Very few dinosaurs were omnivores, that is, animals that ate both meat and plants.

What sounds did dinosaurs make?

It remains a mystery! Palaeontologists are not sure of the kind of sounds that dinosaurs made but their skulls reveal that they did make sounds. Some dinosaurs like the Lambeosaur had crests on their head connected to their breathing tracks. The crests were filled with air when the dinosaur breathed. As air passed through these crests, they might have made loud sounds similar to horns.

Find out

How are the coast redwood trees useful?

Pocket fact

I am bigger!
T. Rex was the scariest of all dinosaurs but Giganotosaurus was even bigger than the T. Rex. It was around 15-metres long and 6-metres tall, and had heavy legs that helped it carry its own body weight, which was more than 8 tons.

What made the scariest dinosaur so scary?

It was the Tyrannosaurus Rex, king of dinosaurs! T. Rex was a powerful meat-eater. Everything about this dinosaur was ferocious—from its massive 40-feet-long body to its 4-feet-long jaw. It had strong thighs and a long, powerful tail that helped it move quickly. Its massive 5-feet-long skull could pierce into the prey and grip its flesh at the same time.

What was the weight of the dinosaurs?

It varied from one kind to another! Not all dinosaurs were giant and heavy beings. Fossil records show that there was a variation in the size and weight of dinosaurs. The heaviest dinosaur, the Argentinosaurus weighed almost 100 tons. That's equivalent to the size of 15 elephants. The lightest-known dinosaur was the bee hummingbird that weighed only 2-4 grams!

Pocket fact

Two sets of ribs!

Some dinosaurs like the Tyrannosaurs Rex and Allosaurus had a second set of ribs called gastral ribs on the underside of their body. This set was supposed to keep their body rigid.

Find out

Find pictures of different dinosaur heads. How are they different?

What was the dinosaur with the biggest head called?

It was the Torosaurus! The Torosaurus was known to have the biggest head among all dinosaurs. It was a horned dinosaur, related to the Triceratops, which lived in the American West, 65 million years ago. It had an 8-feet-long skull, longer than that of any other land animal. The name Torosaurus means "bull lizard".

What kind of teeth did dinosaurs have?

Different dinosaurs had different kinds of teeth! Plant-eating dinosaurs had long, thin, blunt and rake-shaped teeth. They used their teeth to strip leaves off branches. Some dinosaurs had whole rows of grinding teeth to mash up plants. On the other hand, meat-eating dinosaurs had large, pointed and knife-like teeth that helped them rip meat off their prey and swallow it whole.

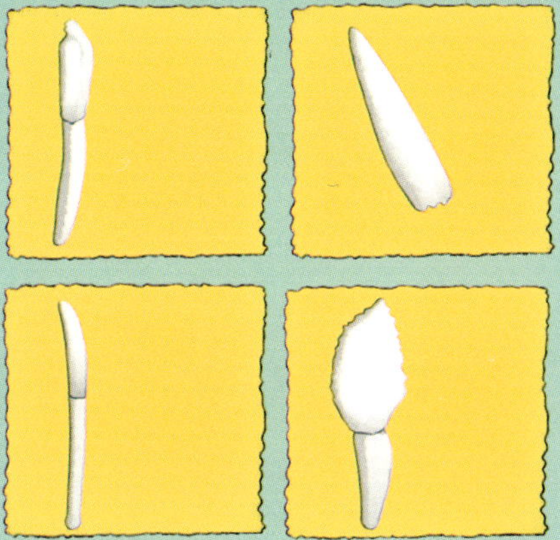

Pocket fact

Five layers!

The teeth of different dinosaurs were made-up of different layers. Triceratops's teeth were made of five layers of tissue. In contrast, the teeth of modern plant-eating animals, such as horses have four layers of tissue.

Try this!

Make a model of the habitats of plant-eating and meat-eating dinosaurs. Compare and list the differences.

What was the habitat of dinosaurs?

It varied from riverside to mixed forests! Different dinosaurs lived at different times and in different parts of the world. Dinosaurs in the Triassic period lived at riversides and in scrublands, while the dinosaurs that lived during the Jurassic Period dwelled in Riparian and dense coniferous forests. In the Cretaceous period, swampland, mixed forests, mountains and desert plains were ideal places for dinosaurs to live.

What was the smallest-known dinosaur?

We know them only by their footprints! The smallest dinosaurs are known only by their footprints. It was believed to be a meat-eater from Nova Scotia and was almost 200 million years old. This dinosaur was assumed to be the size of a little robin. However, later on it was believed that the footprints actually belonged to a baby dinosaur. As for full grown dinosaurs, the smallest are the little bird-hipped plant-eaters like the Lesothosaurus, which were the size of big chickens.

Pocket fact

Thunder thighs!
Researchers from the Sam Noble Museum discovered the enormously powerful thigh muscles, of a dinosaur in Utah, USA. It was named Brontomerus mcintoshi or "thunder thighs".

Find out

Is the thigh bone the longest bone in a dinosaur's body?

What were the fastest dinosaurs called?

The ostrich mimic Ornithomimids! Ornithomimids were toothless meat-eaters with long limbs like those of ostriches. They were the fastest of all dinosaurs. Some dinosaurs of the group, such as the Dromiceiomimus could probably run at speeds of up to 80 kilometres per hour.

What size were the biggest and the smallest dinosaur eggs?

The biggest dinosaur eggs ever found are shaped like giant footballs and are about 19-inches long. They belong to the Segnosaurus, a meat-eating dinosaur that lived in Asia. The smallest dinosaur eggs are just a few inches across and are shaped like tennis balls; however, it is not known which dinosaur laid these eggs.

Try this!

Compare the life cycle of a dinosaur with that of a modern-day reptile.

Pocket fact

Round or elongated?

The eggs laid by meat-eating dinosaurs were much longer than they were wide, while the eggs of Sauropods, Ornithopods, and other plant-eating dinosaurs were found to be more spherical in shape. Palaeontologists are not sure why it was so!

What did dinosaur eggs look like?

They were of different shapes and sizes! Dinosaurs laid eggs, just like reptiles and birds. Some eggs were as small as cannonballs while some as giant as footballs. Most dinosaurs made nests in the sand and laid eggs in them. Their nests were probably covered with plants to keep the eggs warm. Some dinosaurs also looked after their babies, until they were big enough to take care of themselves.

What were the longest dinosaurs called?

It was called the Argentinosaurus! Argentinosaurus huinculensis was a herbivore that belonged to the titanosaur group of dinosaurs. Its fossils were discovered in Argentina in 1987 by a local rancher. Later, Dr. Rodolfo Coria found more fossils of the dinosaur and estimated it to be 110-feet long and 100 tons. That's as long as 3 school buses and as heavy as 20 bulls and elephants. In 1993, he named the dinosaur Argentinosaurus.

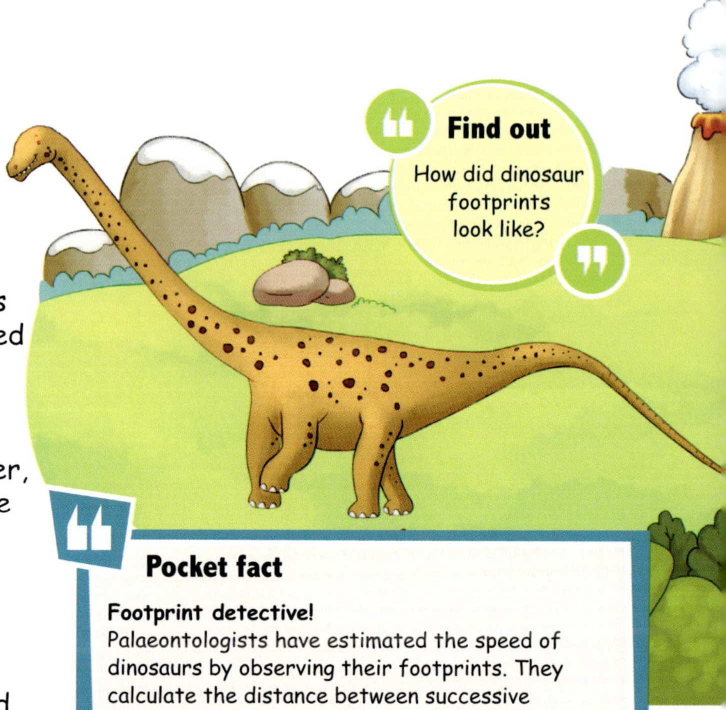

Find out

How did dinosaur footprints look like?

Pocket fact

Footprint detective!
Palaeontologists have estimated the speed of dinosaurs by observing their footprints. They calculate the distance between successive footprints and the distance between prints made by the same foot to estimate the speed.

What was the most brainy dinosaur called?

It was the Troodon! The palaeontologists compare the size of a dinosaur's body to its brain size to get a rough measurement of its intelligence. Based on this, the Troodon has been found to be the smartest of all dinosaurs. It was a meat-eater with a brain as big as an avocado pit. It was not only the smartest dinosaur, but the smartest animal of that existed during that period, including the mammals of the Mesozoic Era.

What was the first dinosaur to be named?

It was the Megalosaurus! William Buckland, a British fossil hunter and clergyman discovered some dinosaur fossils in 1819 and named it Megalosaurus in 1824. It was the first dinosaur to be scientifically described and also the first Theropod dinosaur discovered. Before that dinosaurs had not yet been recognized as a separate taxonomic group—the word dinosaur hadn't even been invented till then!

Find out

Imagine that you have found a dinosaur fossil. Would you like to name it after yourself? What would you name it?

What was the longest name of a dinosaur?

It was Micropachycephalosaurus! It means "tiny thick-headed lizard". It was a herbivore and lived in what is now Shandong, China. Its fossils were discovered in China. Its name was coined by the Chinese palaeontologist Dong in 1978.

Pocket fact

What's the name?
Dinosaurs were not only named on the basis of their behaviour but also after the places where their fossils were found or after the person who discovered them. For example, the Aegyptosaurus was named after Egypt where a few of its fossils have been found.

What was the first-ever mounted dinosaur skeleton like?

It was assembled on an iron latticework! In 1868, the bones of a Hadrosaurus were used to create the first-ever mounted dinosaur skeleton. It was put on display at the Academy of Natural Sciences, then located in Philadelphia, PA. Assembled in a life-like pose, the three-storey-high model was the first dinosaur skeleton ever mounted anywhere in the world.

Pocket fact

What a display!
The American Museum of Natural History has more than 136 dinosaur specimens on view, just a tiny fraction of the largest collection of dinosaurs in the world!

Find out

What do palaeontologists deduce from dinosaur skulls?

What was a dinosaur skull like?

It had many different features! Dinosaur skulls were divided into parts unlike human skulls that are fused into one large bony structure. Also, dinosaur skulls had two pairs of openings, called fenestra, behind the opening for the eye on each side of the skull, and two near the top of the skull. The dinosaur skull also had a jaw with five bones and the hinge that is often at the back of the mandible and usually below the teeth.

What kind of skin did dinosaurs have?

It was scaly! Palaeontologists have found skin fossils which suggest that dinosaur skin was tough and scaly, like that of modern-day reptiles. Some like the Hadrosaurs had tough, wrinkled skin with bony plates. On the other hand, Ornithopods had thick, wrinkled skin with embedded bony knobs of various sizes. Small Theropods, like the Sinosauropteryx, may have had feather-like features on their skin for heat regulation.

Pocket fact

Unique eyes!
The meat-eating dinosaur Carnotaurus had unique eyes that faced forward, rather than to the side like most other dinosaurs.

Find out

Did dinosaurs shed their skin like most present-day reptiles?

What kind of eyes did dinosaurs have?

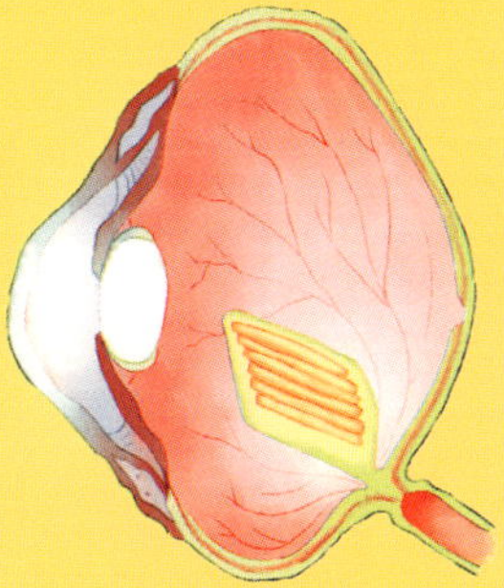

They were of two major kinds! Dinosaurs could be grouped into two categories based on the position of their eyes. The first were Allosauroids, which had eyes pointing laterally, and the second were Coelurosaurs, which had eyes facing forward. Some dinosaurs like the Allosaurus did not have very good binocular vision, compared to modern alligators. On the other hand, dinosaurs like Troodon and Deinonychus had better binocular vision.

What helped dinosaurs watch for danger?

Good vision and sense of smell! Nearly all plant-eating dinosaurs had eyes set high on the sides of their heads. This gave them all-round vision which helped them watch-out for any hint of danger. On the other hand, meat-eating dinosaurs had binocular vision that helped them sense danger from long distances. Dinosaurs also had a good sense of smell that was useful for detecting danger.

Find out

Did dinosaurs feed on smaller reptiles and fish?

Pocket fact

Is it an earthquake!

Some dinosaurs were really huge! The Sauroposeidon, a plant-eating dinosaur was named "earthquake god lizard" because it was believed that when this dinosaur walked, the whole Earth shook due to its size.

What helped dinosaurs digest their food?

It was different for herbivores and carnivores! Both plant-eating and meat-eating dinosaurs ruled the Earth millions of years ago. Many herbivorous dinosaurs swallowed stones that helped them grind their food. Also, they probably relied on the bacteria in their gut to break-down leaves sufficiently to release nutrients. Carnivorous dinosaurs had much shorter digestive tracts than herbivores. They relied on strong stomach acids to break-down their meals.

It was the bone of the Argentinosaurus! The biggest single dinosaur bone ever found was the thigh bone of the Argentinosaurus which was 8-feet long. It was discovered by Diego Pol in the desert of Central Argentina.

> **Pocket fact**
>
> **What a price!**
> A huge T. Rex fossil was found by fossil hunter Sue Hendrickson in 1990. The Chicago Museum purchased this famous Tyrannosaurus Sue fossil for $8 million.

> **Find out**
>
> When did humans appear on Earth?

What happened after dinosaurs became extinct?

The world changed a lot! It is estimated that 75% or more of all species on Earth vanished with the extinction of dinosaurs. Yet many new forms evolved on Earth, which included flowering plants; mammals such as horses, whales, bats; and primates. Birds, fish, lizards also came into being.

When?

When did dinosaurs rule the Earth?

About 200 million years ago! Dinosaurs were a group of reptiles that lived during the Mesozoic Era, which began 245 million years ago. They were the dominant life-forms on Earth for nearly 180 million years. But they faced a sudden extinction at the end of the Cretaceous period, about 65 million years ago.

> **Pocket fact**
>
> **A large number!**
> Around 1,543–2,468 dinosaur species existed on Earth during the Mesozoic Era.

> **Find out**
>
> What was the Earth like when dinosaurs lived on it?

When was the first dinosaur fossil found?

Way back in 1676! Robert Plot the curator of an English museum found a thigh bone that he thought belonged to a giant. But that fossil disappeared without a trace. Later on, in 1822, Mary Ann Mantell and her husband Gideon discovered the large teeth of the herbivorous reptile Iguanodon, in England.

When was the name 'dinosaur' coined?

In 1841! Richard Owen, an English biologist, anatomist and palaeontologist is remembered for coining the word *Dinosauria*, meaning "Terrible Reptile" or "Fearfully Great Reptile". He published an important general account of the land reptiles of the Mesozoic Era and stated that dinosaur fossils were distinct from the teeth or bones of any living creature; and hence he named the group Dinosauria. He divided them into three categories—the carnivorous Megalosaurus, the herbivorous Iguanodon and the armoured Hylaeosaurus.

Find out

Did dinosaurs sit on their eggs as birds do today?

Pocket fact

Dawn Stealer!
The earliest named dinosaur was the meat-eating Eoraptor and its name means "dawn stealer". It was named so because it lived at the dawn of the Dinosaur Age.

When were the massive eggs of Therizinosaurus found?

In 2011! A nursery of Therizinosaurus was found in the Gobi Desert in Mongolia by the palaeontologist Yoshitsugu Kobayashi and his colleagues. The nesting colony had 17 clutches of eggs. The eggs were round and 5-inches in diameter with rough outer shells. The eggs did not harbour dinosaur embryos but many of them had holes with eggshells inside. It seemed as if a baby dinosaur had poked a hole in the egg and the broken shells had fallen back inside.

When was the nearly-complete skeleton of a dinosaur found?

In 1988! The fossil of a nearly-complete skeleton of a bipedal dinosaur named Herrerasaurus was found in north-western Argentina in the foothills of the Andes. Herrerasaurus was one of the earliest dinosaurs that lived 231 million years ago. The fragments of this fossil were discovered by Victorino Herrera, an Andean goatherd, in 1959. However, it was in 1988 that Alfredo Monetta discovered the rest of the bones of the Herrerasaurus, and this gave the researchers a complete picture of the dinosaur.

> **Pocket fact**
>
> **Double hinged!**
> The Herrerasaurus had a long pointed head with sharp teeth enclosed in a double-hinged jaw. The joints in the jaw allowed the Herrerasaurus to grip its prey.

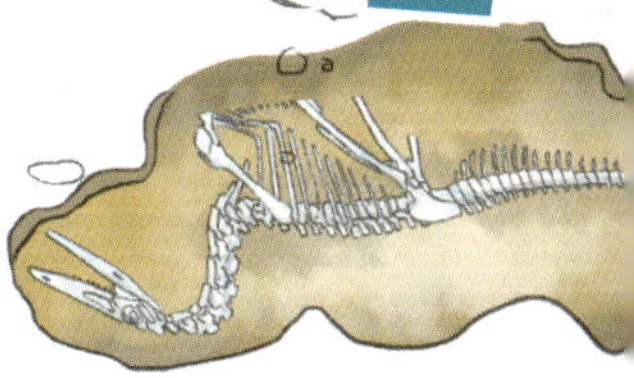

> **Find out**
>
> Was Coelophysis a herbivore or a carnivore?

When were hundreds of Coelophysis skeletons discovered?

In 1947! Edwin H. Colbert, curator of fossil reptiles at the American Museum of Natural History, was on an expedition to the Baldwin's Coelophysis site with his team. It was on this expedition that fossil preparatory George Whitaker found a bone-bed of hundreds of Coelophysis skeletons in the red Triassic rocks at Ghost Ranch near Abiquiu, New Mexico. This discovery made Coelophysis a popular dinosaur.

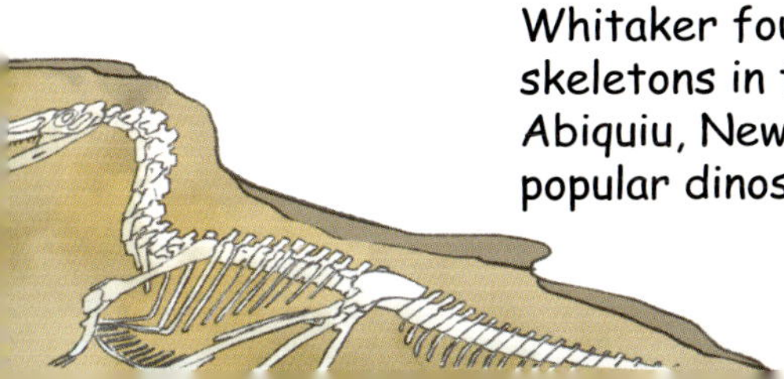

When did the first giant dinosaur appear on Earth?

222-215 million years ago! Dinosaurs were not the first living things that roamed the Earth. Reptiles like Archosaurus, Pterosaurus and Desmatosuchus lived on Earth before dinosaurs came into existence. The appearance of dinosaurs dates back to the late Triassic period. Chindesaurus and Coelophysis were one of the earliest-known dinosaurs and they were around 6-8 feet in length. However, the first giant dinosaurs, the Plateosauruses, were around 26-feet long and 3-4 metres high.

Find out

Which was the largest known Sauropod?

Pocket fact

Before the dinosaurs! Plateosaurus fossils were first discovered in France in 1837. It was actually named before dinosaurs were recognized as a group.

When did Sauropods appear on Earth?

In the Late Triassic Era! Sauropods were lizard-hipped dinosaurs with very long necks, long tails, small heads (as compared to their body) and four thick, pillar-like legs. They were known for the huge sizes attained by some species. They were diversely and abundantly found 150-120 million years ago, during the Late Jurassic and Early Cretaceous periods.

When did Theropods live on Earth?

From the Late Triassic Era through the latest Cretaceous Era! Theropods were ancestrally carnivores but later they evolved to become herbivores, omnivores, piscivores and insectivores. They first appeared approximately 231.4 million years ago. Theropods included a wide range of dinosaurs—from the smallest-known adult Mesozoic non-avian dinosaur to the great Tyrannosaurus and Giganotosaurus.

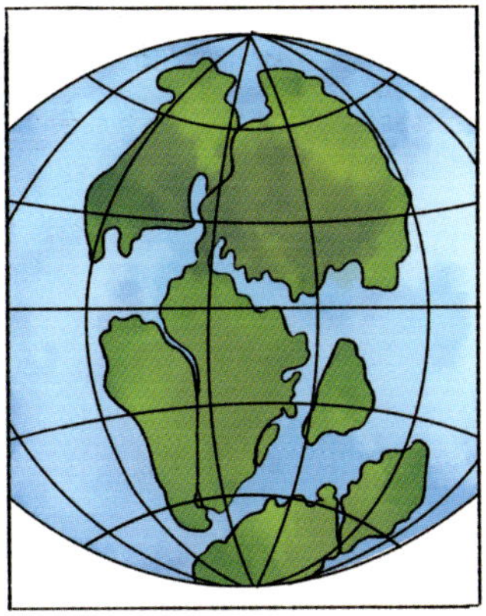

Find out

What was the size of a T. Rex's skull?

Pocket fact

I am the smallest!
Hesperonychus was the smallest-known North American carnivorous dinosaur. It was about 1-metre long. It ate insects, baby dinosaurs and small Cretaceous animals.

When did the 'King of Dinosaurs' evolve?

In the late Jurassic period! The Jurassic period extended from 201 million to 145 million years ago. T. Rex, the king of dinosaurs appeared on Earth about 150 million years ago. It was a large meat-eating dinosaur, with very large, high skulls that were over 3 feet long. It weighed around 4000–7000 kg and was approximately 14-metres long.

When did dinosaurs gather together in groups?

While hunting and also when they wanted to stay safe! Palaeontologists have found many dinosaur fossils which show social groups. It is assumed that plant-eaters (like Hypsilophodons) might have gathered in groups to protect themselves from their predators. On the other hand, carnivorous dinosaurs (like the Velociraptors) may have formed groups while hunting for food.

Try it!

What name would you like to use for a group of Diplodocuses?

Pocket fact

Human-like fingers!
The Iguanodon was not only known for its size and ungainly posture but also for its fingers. The most notable features of the Iguanodon were its hind limbs that were equipped with five fingers. Three of its middle fingers were bound together with flesh whereas the fourth finger and thumb were able to move freely.

When was the first herd of dinosaur skeletons found?

In 1878! The first big hoard of skeletons was found 322 metres underground in a coal mine in Bernissart, Belgium. Miners were digging at 322 metres when they came across 32 Iguanodon skeletons in life-like poses, encrusted with pyrite. The discovery was reported to the Belgian Royal Museum of Natural History (as it was then known) on 12 April 1878.

When was the smallest fossilized dinosaur skeleton found?

In the 1970s! The smallest fossilized dinosaur skeleton ever found was that of a baby Mussaurus's skull. Mussaurus was a small, plant-eating dinosaur. Palaeontologists have not found any adult Mussaurus fossils yet. During the 1970s, Jose Bonaparte, who was leading an expedition to the El Tranquilo Formation, discovered fragmented juvenile fossils, skulls and dinosaur eggs. The skulls of the baby dinosaurs were so small that they could fit on a fingertip!

Find out

How many dinosaur fossils are there in the Dinosaur National Park?

Pocket fact

Thin egg shells!
Mussaurus' eggs are known for having unusually thin shells as compared to most long-necked dinosaurs whose eggs had much thicker shells.

When were 300 tons of dinosaur bones found?

In 1909! A palaeontologist, Earl Douglass was hunting for dinosaur fossils in Utah, USA, when he found eight tailbones of an Apatosaurus protruding from a sandstone hill in the Utah desert. This eventually led him to the discovery of a dinosaur quarry where approximately 300 tons of dinosaur bones were found. In 1915, the Dinosaur National Monument was established in Utah to protect and conserve this dinosaur quarry.

When did the Ankylosaurus swing its club?

When it sensed danger! Ankylosaurus was a heavily armoured dinosaur that lived during the late Cretaceous period, about 65.5 million to 66.8 million years ago. It had a large club-like protrusion at the end of its tail. Ankylosaurus swung its club to hit its attackers. Alternatively, it may have been used for display purposes, such as for attracting mates.

Pocket fact

Fused lizard!

The name Ankylosaurus means "fused lizard". The dinosaur was named so because it had fused bones in its skull and other parts of its body. These bones gave the Ankylosaurus a rugged appearance, similar to a crocodile.

Find out

When and by whom was Troodon first discovered?

When did a Troodon usually hunt for its prey?

At night! Troodon was a small, bird-like, meat-eating dinosaur that lived 76 million years ago, during the Campanian age of the Cretaceous period. It was considered to be one of the most intelligent dinosaurs, given the size of its brain. Palaeontologists believe that Troodon had large, forward-facing eyes and vertical pupils that granted it keen vision for hunting, even at night.

When did a dinosaur fossil irritate its finders?

When they were unable to reconstruct its original features! Irritator was a dinosaur that lived around 105–110 million years ago, during the early Cretaceous period. Its only known fossil, an 80-cm skull was discovered in 1996 by palaeontologists Martill, Cruikshank, Frey, Small and Clarke. The fossil was badly masked by plaster, by illegal fossil hunters, making the snout appear longer. This made it difficult for the palaeontologists to reconstruct its original features and thus it was named Irritator—a name which comes from the word irritated.

Pocket fact

Not always static!
Dinosaur names are not always static. The giant Apatosaurus was initially named so by palaeontologist Othniel C. Marsh. Later on, similar but larger bones of the Apatosaurus were found and so the dinosaur's name was changed to Brontosaurus. However, eventually, it was decided that the first-decided name "Apatosaurus" should be retained.

When was the first dinosaur brain discovered?

In 2004! The first fossilized dinosaur brain was discovered by amateur fossil hunter Jamie Hiscocks in Surrey, England. The brain belonged to the plant-eating dinosaur, Bexhill iguanodontian that roamed, in Sussex, England, a little over 130 million years ago. This is one of the most amazing dinosaur discoveries because of the rarity of the preservation of the soft-tissue of the dinosaur brain.

Find out

How do palaeontologists preserve fossils?

When did the "Bone Wars" begin?

In 1870! The "Bone Wars" also known as the "Great Dinosaur Rush" refers to a period of intense fossil discovery by two palaeontologists. Edward Drinker Cope of the Academy of Natural Sciences, Philadelphia and Othniel Charles Marsh of Peabody Museum of Natural History, faced off in a very peculiar struggle. They competed to determine who could find more dinosaur bones and species. During this period, around 130 species were identified between the two rivals. The "Bone Wars" ended in 1897 with the death of Edward Drinker Cope.

Find out

Who won the "Bone Wars" and why?

Pocket fact

It's interesting!
Many interesting dinosaur fossils have been discovered by palaeontologists till date. One of the most interesting fossils was that of the dinosaur Citipati shielding her eggs!

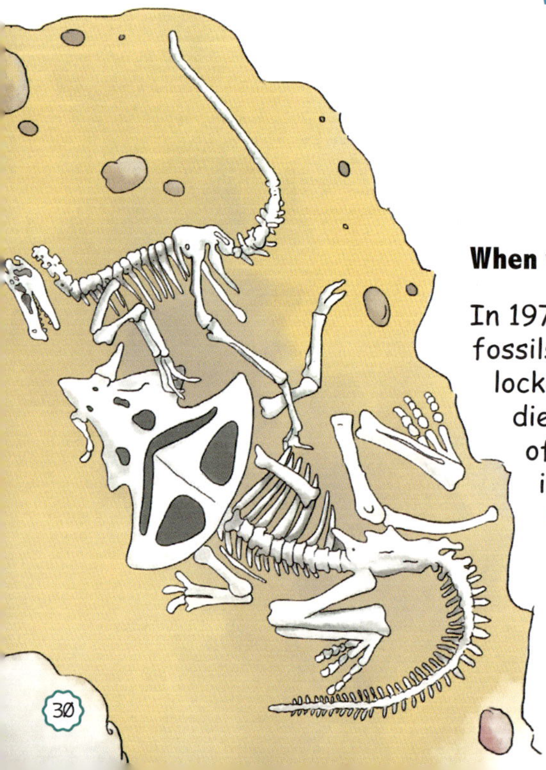

When was the 'Fighting Dinosaurs' fossil found?

In 1971! A Polish-Mongolian team discovered the fossils of a Velociraptor and a Protoceratops locked in combat, with both dinosaurs having died at the same time. The fossil shows one of the Velociraptor's foot claws lodged into the Protoceratops' neck, and the Protoceratops seems to have bit down and broken one of the Velociraptor's arms. This discovery showed that predatory dinosaurs hunted and scavenged the plant-eating dinosaurs.

When was the first Velociraptor fossil discovered?

In 1923! Velociraptor was a theropod dinosaur that lived approximately 75-71 million years ago, during the later part of the Cretaceous period. Palaeontologist Peter Kaisen discovered the Velociraptor fossil on the first American Museum of Natural History expedition to the Outer Mongolian Gobi Desert. The fossil consisted of a complete but crushed skull and a toe claw.

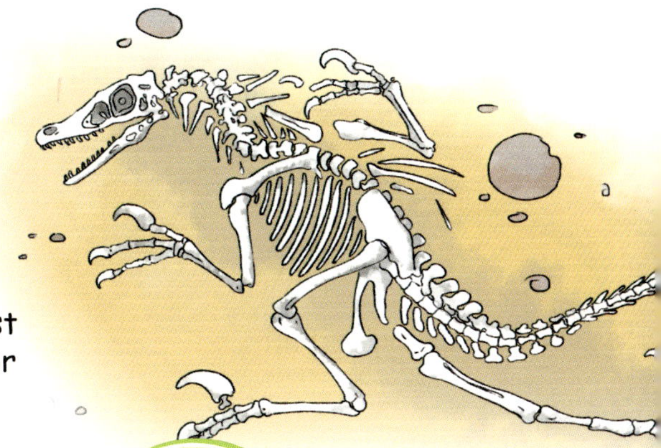

Find out

Why did the Stegosaurus have a throat guard?

Pocket fact

Two Species!

So far only two species of the Velociraptor have been discovered. One is Velociraptor mongoliensis, named in 1924 and the other is Velociraptor osmolskae, which was discovered in 2008.

When was the Stegosaurus declared the state fossil of Colorado?

In 1982! Stegosaurus was a large herbivorous dinosaur that lived in the area now called Colorado, 150 million years ago. The first Stegosaurus fossil was discovered in 1876, in Colorado, by M.P. Felch. Approximately 80 more fossils were discovered in the coming years. The fossils were declared the official state fossils of Colorado, in 1982, as a tribute to the number of dinosaur skeletons found in the state.

When was the first longest dinosaur fossil found?

In 1877! Diplodocus was the longest of all known dinosaurs. The first Diplodocus fossil was found near Cañon City, Colorado in 1877. It was discovered by Benjamin Mudge and Samuel W. Williston, and was named by Othniel Charles Marsh in 1878. A number of Diplodocus fossils have also been found in the Rocky Mountain region of Colorado, Montana, Utah and Wyoming.

Pocket fact

Laying eggs!
In a surprising discovery, the palaeontologists discovered the eggs of the Diplodocuses in lines, rather than in nests. This suggests that these long Sauropods may have laid eggs while they walked along!

Find out

Which movie was entirely dedicated to dinosaurs? Which dinosaur was the most featured in this movie?

When was the 'different lizard' discovered?

In 1877! Allosaurus, meaning 'different lizard,' was first discovered in Colorado in 1877, by palaeontologist Othniel Charles Marsh. This specimen comprised just a few fragments of the dinosaur's bones. These fragments were initially named Antrodemus and the family of these large theropods was named Allosauridae. But a study of the abundant remains from the Cleveland-Lloyd Dinosaur Quarry brought the name "Allosaurus" back to prominence.

When was Dromaeosaurus discovered?

In 1914! The Dromaeosaurus was a small sized, lightly-built dinosaur that belonged to the family Dromaeosauridae. It flourished in Asia and North America during the Cretaceous period. The fossils of the Dromaeosaurus were first discovered by palaeontologist Barnum Brown, in the year 1914, along the banks of the Red Deer River of Alberta. In 1922, William Diller Matthew and Brown named this species—Dromaeosaurus albertensis. The generic name dromeus means 'runner' and sauros means 'lizard'. The specific name, "albertensis", refers to Alberta.

Pocket fact

The Alvarez hypothesis!

The theory that the impact of a large asteroid hitting the Earth caused the mass extinction of dinosaurs and many other living things, was termed the Alvarez hypothesis. It is named after the father-and-son team of scientists, Luis and Walter Alvarez, who first suggested it in 1980.

Find out

How long was the Dromaeosaurus?

When did the rule of dinosaurs end?

About 65 million years ago! Dinosaurs ruled the Earth throughout the Mesozoic Era, approximately 245 million years ago, and vanished from Earth approximately 65 million years ago. The cause of their extinction remains a mystery with many reasons stated, such as climatic change, diseases, changing plant communities and geologic events. The most accepted theory is that a large asteroid struck the Earth, off the northern tip of the Yucatan Peninsula of Mexico; thus ending the rule of dinosaurs on Earth.

How?

How do we get to know about dinosaurs?

By studying fossils! We know all about dinosaurs from the fossils which survived over the millennium. Fossils are remains (bones) or impressions of prehistoric plants or animals embedded in rocks. Palaeontologists have found fossilized bones of dinosaurs and have reconstructed these bones to find out what dinosaurs looked like, how they moved and even, what they ate.

Pocket fact

The first dinosaur bone!
The first dinosaur bone was found in England, in 1676, by Robert Plot. At the time, he believed that the bone belonged to a "giant," but later on it was identified as a dinosaur bone. The first dinosaur bone to be found belonged to the Megalosaurus.

Find out

Who proposed the method to classify dinosaurs?

How many types of dinosaurs are known?

Hundreds of them! At present, over 700 different species of dinosaurs have been identified and named by palaeontologists. Also, these species have been divided into two groups named Saurischia (lizard hipped) and Ornithischia (bird hipped).

How are dinosaurs named?

Usually, dinosaurs are named after a characteristic body feature, after the place where they were found or after a person who discovered their fossils. A dinosaur's name consists of two Greek or Latin words (or combinations). The genus name is written first followed by the species name. For example, the name T. Rex is a combination of both Latin and Greek words, and means "King of the tyrant lizards".

> **Pocket fact**
>
> **First found!**
> The first Dilophosaurus specimens were found by Sam Welles in 1942, in the Kayenta Formation in Arizona. The site was discovered by a Navajo, Jesse Williams, in 1940.

> **Try this!**
>
> If you were to re-name the T. Rex and Dilophosaurus, which names would you like to use?

How did Dilophosaurus get its name?

From its skull! Dilophosaurus was a carnivore that lived in the early Jurassic period, around 190 million years ago. Dilophosaurus had an unusual feature—a pair of crests on its skull. It is from this feature that it gets its name, which means "two-crested lizard".

How long could a dinosaur live?

It varied from one dinosaur species to another! The lifespan of an animal relates in part to its body size and metabolism. Palaeontologists observed growth rings in the fossil bones of dinosaurs. Similar to tree rings, each ring in a dinosaur bone marks another year of growth. These rings show that the large herbivorous dinosaurs, such as the Brachiosaurs and Diplodocus, would have lived for 70–80 years whereas the smaller, meat-eating dinosaurs had a lifespan of 20–30 years.

Pocket fact

The largest-known dinosaur egg is smaller than the egg of the extinct Elephant bird of Madagascar.

Find out

How small was the smallest dinosaur egg ever found?

How were dinosaur babies born?

They hatched from eggs! Unlike mammals, dinosaurs did not give birth to their young ones; the female dinosaurs laid eggs, just like most reptiles and birds do. The study of fossils shows that some dinosaurs made nests using twigs and leaves, or dug holes in the soil or sand to place their eggs. A baby dinosaur may have pecked its way out of its protective shell with a specially designed egg tooth, just like baby birds do.

How did dinosaurs move about?

They walked and ran! Different dinosaurs moved around in different ways. Some walked on four legs (these are known as quadrupeds), and some on two legs (these are called bipeds). There were other dinosaurs that may have used two legs to run but they still walked and grazed on four legs. A few of the bird-like dinosaurs may have used their short, feathered arms to help speed up their running and perhaps to glide from trees to the ground. Dinosaurs probably used their tails for balance while moving and making quick turns.

Pocket fact

The fastest ones!
The fastest dinosaurs were the bird-like, bipedal carnivores (theropods) with long, slim hind-limbs and light bodies.

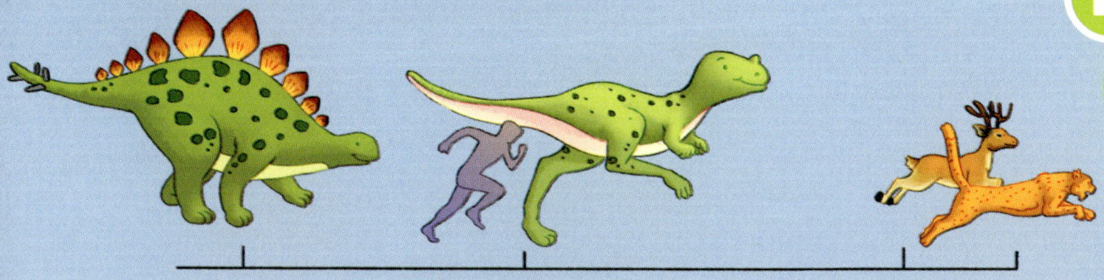

Find out

Were there any dinosaurs that could swim?

How fast could dinosaurs walk or run?

Dinosaurs lived several years before human beings came into existence, so it is difficult to estimate how fast they walked or ran. However, scientists have suggested a formula to measure fossil footprints and the size of the dinosaur's leg to estimate the speed of some dinosaurs. As per the calculations based on this formula, the fastest dinosaurs were the ornithomimids, which ran at a speed of 25 mph. The walking-speed of medium-sized, two-legged dinosaurs varied from 4 kph to 6 kph, and for fast running dinosaurs, speed estimates were 37 kph to 88 kph.

How did dinosaurs fly?

They couldn't fly! The legs of dinosaurs were positioned under their bodies rather than out of the sides of their bodies (like that of crocodiles). So, what you might have assumed were flying dinosaurs were actually flying reptiles, known as pterosaurs. Examples of pterosaurs are Pteranodon and Pterodactylus. Aside from prehistoric insects, pterosaurs were the first-known flying reptiles.

Pocket fact

I weigh 100 grams!
Not all flying reptiles were huge like the giant dinosaurs. A pterosaur named Peteinosaurus, had a wingspan of less than 1 metre and weighed just 100 grams.

Find out

Where do palaeontologists look for dinosaur fossils?

How do scientists know if they've found a dinosaur bone?

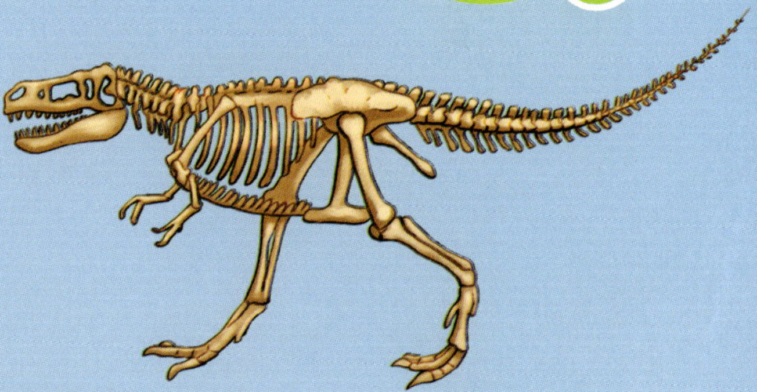

By comparing the shape of the bones with the other dinosaur fossils. Palaeontologists can identify the dinosaur bones on the basis of their size and characteristics. For example, dinosaur bones are usually larger than the bones of other animals belonging to the Jurassic age and they look different, particularly the skull and the pelvis. Also, meat-eating dinosaurs had hollow bones that were, usually, thicker than those of other birds or pterosaurs.

How many teeth did dinosaurs have?

The number varied from fifty to hundreds of them! The T. Rex had around 50-60 thick, conical, bone-crunching teeth. While the Hadrosaurus had the most number of teeth, up to 1000 cheek teeth that were like grinding machines. Unlike humans who only get two sets of teeth in their lifetime, a dinosaur's teeth would re-grow every time it lost them.

Pocket fact

I can't chew!

The dinosaur Apatosaurus had teeth but it couldn't chew. The American Museum of Natural History states that the Apatosaurus had "stripper teeth" that just removed leaves from branches. The dinosaur just swallowed plants whole without chewing.

Find out

When were the first dinosaur teeth fossils discovered?

How big was T. Rex's longest tooth?

About 12 inches long! T. Rex had a mouth full of serrated teeth. But not all of the T. Rex's teeth were long and served the same function. The front teeth of a T. Rex gripped and pulled, its side teeth tore flesh and its back teeth diced chunks of meat and forced food into its throat. The T. Rex had wide and dull teeth, rather than flat and dagger-like, which allowed the teeth to withstand the forces exerted by the struggling prey.The longest T. Rex tooth ever found was about 12 inches (30 centimeters) long.

How was the Spinosaurus different from the other dinosaurs?

Find out

How did the Spinosaurus get its name?

Its size and some of its specific features made it different from the other dinosaurs! Spinosaurus was the biggest of all carnivorous dinosaurs and it mostly ate fish. Most meat-eating dinosaurs had curved teeth but the Spinosaurus had powerful jaws with straight teeth. It lived on both land and water and is said to be the only true aquatic swimming dinosaur. This dinosaur had an amazing sail made from spike-shaped bones, joined together by a layer of skin, on its back, hence the name Spinosaurus.

Pocket fact

Is there danger?
The Triceratops had a frill around its neck. It used this thin flap of skin to signal the other members of its herd of danger. This frill also helped the dinosaur regulate its body temperature.

How many horns did Triceratops have?

Three! Triceratops was a huge plant-eating dinosaur from the late Cretaceous. Triceratops gets its name from the three horns present on its head. However, it actually had only two proper horns which could grow up to 3 feet long. The third horn was made out of soft proteins and wasn't a proper horn. It is said that the dinosaur used its horns to protect itself from danger.

How did dinosaurs turn into fossils?

When they died and got buried in mud and sand! Fossils are the remains or impressions of a prehistoric plant or animal embedded in rock. When dinosaurs died and got buried in mud or sand, the soft parts of their body were decomposed, leaving only the bones. Minerals from the mud soaked into the bones and gradually these minerals started replacing the bones. This turned the bones into fossils.

Find out

Which was the most ferocious dinosaur?

How did dinosaurs protect themselves from danger?

Different dinosaurs used different methods of defence! Some dinosaurs had sharp teeth, claws and whip-like tails that they used as weapons while other dinosaurs, like the Ceratosaurus, had horns for self defence. For speedy dinosaurs, being able to out-run a predator was their main means of protection. Large Sauropods used their size to frighten their enemies. On the other hand, the dinosaurs that did not have horns or spines may have relied on camouflage to protect themselves.

Pocket fact

Dug up!
The word fossil comes from the Latin word *fossilis*, which means, "dug up". Fossils are mostly excavated from sedimentary rock layers.

How are dinosaurs grouped?

On the basis of their bones! Scientists have classified dinosaurs into two groups on the basis of the structure of their bones. The most important difference between these two groups lies in the shape of their hip joints. Dinosaurs with pelvic hips, such as those of lizards, are called Saurischia. While, the second group called Ornithischia, comprises dinosaurs that have hip bones, similar to those of birds.

Find out

Which was the biggest plant-eating dinosaur?

Pocket fact

Two names!
T. Rex was mistakenly named both "Tyrannosaurus Rex" and "Dynamosaurus imperiosus" by palaeontologist H.F. Osborn in his 1905 paper, after he found two fossils. He later realized that they were one and the same.

How were plant-eating dinosaurs different from meat eaters?

There were many features that made them different! Plant-eating or herbivorous dinosaurs usually had long necks which helped them reach the tree tops and munch on the tree leaves. Most of them walked on four legs. They had horns, bony frills, plates, spikes, clubs and long tails. Their teeth were flat. On the other hand, meat-eating or carnivorous dinosaurs had sharp teeth and claws. Most carnivorous dinosaurs stood on two legs so that they could run fast to catch their prey.

How were dinosaurs different from other reptiles?

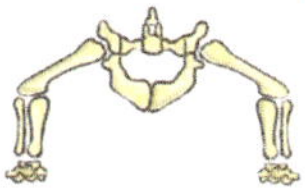

The difference lies mainly in the bones! Though dinosaurs were a part of a large group of reptiles, they were quite different from the present day reptiles. Reptiles have two vertebrae in their hips whereas dinosaurs had five. Reptiles, such as lizards and crocodiles, have their thigh bones almost parallel to the ground, with legs that sprawl out to the side, enabling a side-to-side motion. Dinosaurs, on the other hand, had a hole in their hip socket that helped them stand straight. This posture also allowed dinosaurs to run faster and with greater endurance than other reptiles of the same size.

Find out

How heavy was the heaviest dinosaur?

Pocket fact

We are a part of this group! The dinosaurs were a part of a large group of reptiles called the Archosaurs. The word Archosaurs means 'ruling lizard'.

How is the weight of dinosaurs measured?

It's not measured but estimated! The estimates are made by comparing the size of the dinosaurs with those of the similar present day animals. The estimates are made based on the width of the skeleton, the heaviness of the bones and the size of the dents in the bones where the muscles were joined to it. This also helps scientists to estimate the weight of a dinosaur's muscles.

How did dinosaurs communicate?

Dinosaurs probably communicated both vocally and visually. Dinosaurs such as Corythosaurus and Parasaurolophus had chambered head-crests which they might have used to grunt or bellow. Dinosaurs may have also used their horns, frills and crests for mating rituals or to intimidate rivals.

Find out

Which was the most intelligent dinosaur?

Pocket fact

It's the EQ!
Palaeontologists measure an animal's intelligence on the basis of EQ or Encephalization Quotient. EQ is the ratio of actual brain weight to the predicted brain mass for an animal of a given size.

How big was a dinosaur's brain?

Some were walnut-sized and some the size of a tennis ball! Many of us are under the assumption that huge dinosaurs had large brains but this is not true! The size of the brain varied from one dinosaur to another. Troodon, a meat-eating dinosaur was as big as a man, with a brain the size of an avocado pit. Stegosaurus was a tiny-brained dinosaur, compared to its size. Its brain was the size of a walnut and its body was the size of a truck!

How fast could dinosaurs grow?

They showed yearly periods of rapid and slow growth! Earlier palaeontologists generally assumed that dinosaurs grew slowly and required 50–100 years to attain their great size. But a recent study of growth lines in the fossil bones reveals that dinosaurs grew rapidly in their first years and then showed slow growth. Can you believe that the huge T. Rex grew to its full size, attaining a weight of 10,000 pounds, in 18 years? In order to obtain its immense size and weight, it could put on almost five pounds a day during its phase of maximum growth!

Pocket fact

From short to long!

Dinosaurs were found in different sizes—as tiny as rabbits to as massive as trucks lined together. The Micropachycephalosaurus had a long name but was just the size of a rabbit. On the other hand, the Antarctosaurus was about 59-feet long.

Find out

Which group of dinosaurs did the Baryonyx belong to?

How was Baryonyx a special dinosaur?

It shared many characteristics with crocodiles. Baryonyx is one of the strangest dinosaurs, yet discovered. It was a massive hunter that lived in or near water and hunted fish and other small animals. It had about 90 short teeth which lined its long mouth. Its most distinctive feature was a very large claw (about 12-inches long), which could be used both for protection against enemies as well as a useful tool for hunting.

How are birds and dinosaurs similar?

There were several similarities between birds and dinosaurs. Palaeontologists have found some dinosaur fossils that look almost exactly like birds. It seems these dinosaurs had hollow bones, similar hips, similar hands (modified as wings in birds, but same skeletal structure) and feet. Some other similar characteristics include their skull structure and the fact that they walk on two legs.

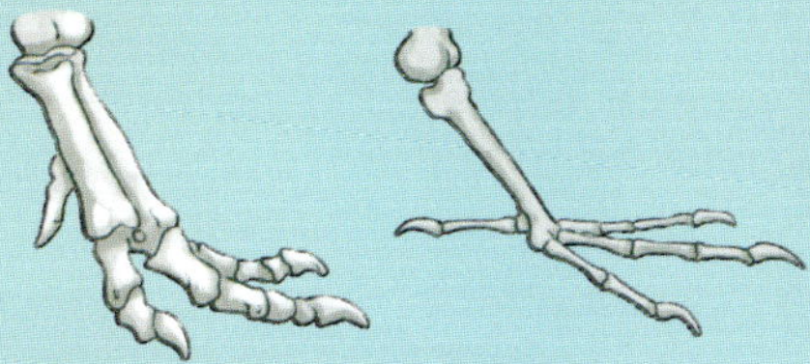

Pocket fact

The ancient wing!
Archaeopteryx which first appeared in the Jurassic period had the features of both birds and dinosaurs. It had a toothed jaw, clawed fingers, a long bony tail like a dinosaur but it also had a beak, wings and feathers like a bird.

Find out

Were dinosaurs cold-blooded like reptiles or warm-blooded like mammals?

How were pterosaurs and dinosaurs different?

Pterosaurs were flying reptiles that flourished during the time when dinosaurs lived. Pterosaurs were quite different from dinosaurs. Most pterosaurs had elongated jaws with needle-like teeth. Some of them also had a beak but lacked teeth. On the other hand, dinosaurs couldn't fly and each kind of dinosaur had different types of teeth. Plant-eating dinosaurs had flat teeth while meat-eating dinosaurs had sharp teeth. Also, pterosaurs are more closely related to birds than to reptiles.

Why?

Why do dinosaurs usually have 'saur' in their name?

Saur means 'a lizard'! Dinosaurs were huge animals that lived millions of years ago. We get to know about dinosaurs by studying their fossils. When dinosaur fossils were first discovered by Robert Owen, he used the word dinosaur by combining the Greek words deinos, which means `terrible,' and sauros, which means `lizard'. Dinosaurs were thought to be gigantic versions of lizards, hence the use of 'saur' in their name.

> **Pocket fact**
>
> **Spiky tail!**
> The thagomizer is an arrangement of spikes at the end of a dinosaur's tail. The term was coined by Gary Larson in a 1982 Far Side comic.

> **Find out**
>
> Take some play dough and make a dinosaur model of your own. What would you like to name your dinosaur?

Why do palaeontologists dig dinosaur bones?

To find out more about dinosaurs! Palaeontologists are scientists who study fossils, that is the bones and remains of animals that were buried long ago. They keep careful records of the fossils they find and use this information later to identify the different types of dinosaurs and their habitats. By studying fossils, palaeontologists also get to know how things change under certain conditions and this helps them understand the relative magnitude of changes happening in today's world.

Why was T. Rex different from the other dinosaurs?

It had the strongest bite! Tyrannosaurus Rex was one of the largest meat-eating dinosaurs that ever lived. Its name means "the king of the tyrant lizards". This meat-eater was about 40 feet long and around 15–20 feet tall. It had a huge head with large, pointed, replaceable teeth and well-developed jaw muscles. Apart from its size, what made this dinosaur different from the others was its bite. Its bite could exert a force of up to 12,814 pounds, which is roughly equivalent to the force of a medium-sized elephant sitting down!

Find out

Which dinosaur had a spike on each hand?

Pocket fact

What a bite!

T. Rex is said to have had the most powerful bite of all! Its jaw exerted a crushing 3.6 tonnes of force, equivalent to the weight of three mid-sized cars.

Why did T. Rex leave small footprints although its feet were much longer?

Because it walked on its toes! Tyrannosaurus Rex, the huge meat-eating dinosaur lived about 85–65 million years ago. It had puny arms, but its feet were more impressive—almost 3.3 feet long. However, the T. Rex left only 1.55 feet-long footprints (even though its feet were much longer) because unlike humans, the T. Rex's heels did not touch the ground while walking!

Why does Stegosaurus have plates on its back?

To regulate heat! Stegosaurus was a large, plant-eating dinosaur that lived during the late Jurassic Period, about 150.8–155.7 million years ago. The most impressive features of the Stegosaurus were the two rows of bony plates, called scutes, along its back. The Stegosaurus' plates were embedded with a network of blood vessels and were probably used to regulate its body heat. It is believed that these plates would absorb light from the Sun during the day and dissipate extra body heat at night, thus controlling the Stegosaurus' body temperature.

Pocket fact

A lump in the tail!
The dinosaur Euoplocephalus had a tail with a bony lump. It swung its tail to hit its enemy with such a great force that it could break its bones!

Try this!

Work in pairs. Act as a Troodon and ask your friend to act as its prey. Play hide and seek. What senses did you use to hunt for your prey?

Why was Troodon also known as 'Wounding Tooth'?

Because of its saw-like teeth! Troodon was a small bird-like dinosaur from the Cretaceous period. The dinosaur was named so by palaeontologist Joseph Leidy who discovered a single serrated tooth belonging to it in Montana during the 1850s. The Troodon's teeth were different from those of most other theropods, as they bore prominent apically oriented serrations. These "wounding" serrations suggest that the dinosaur had a possibly omnivorous diet; and hence it got the name "wounding Tooth".

Why was the Diplodocus also called 'Old Whip-Tail'?

Because it had a whip-like tail! Diplodocus was a long-necked dinosaur, about 90-feet long with a whip-like tail that was 45-feet long. Diplodocus is also known as 'Old Whip-Tail' because it could swish its tail so hard that it made a crack like a whip! This would scare off its enemies.

Find out

What did the Spinosaurus eat?

Pocket fact

I am a big baby!
Newly hatched Diplodocus babies only weigh a few kilograms. However, they grow by one ton a year until they are adults. That's an astonishing 2-3 kilograms a day! By the time they are one-year-old, they measure almost 3 meters long and weigh as much as a full-grown horse.

Why do scientists say that the Spinosaurus lived in water?

It had some features that support aquatic life! The Spinosaurus was a large meat-eating dinosaur with a long sail on its back. It is the only known dinosaur that is said to have dwelled in water. Its nostrils were further up on its snout compared to that of the other dinosaurs. This would have allowed it to breathe even with most of its snout submerged ir water. It had crocodile-like teeth that were ideal for catching fish. It also had paddle-like webbed feet that would've allowed the dinosaur to swim.

Why were Velociraptors compared to birds?

Because they had a lot in common with birds! Velociraptor was covered with feathers, had hollow bones, wishbones and also brooded their nests just like birds. Velociraptors also had quill knobs—places where the quills of the wing feathers of modern birds are anchored to the bone. If Velociraptors were alive today they would be considered as very unusual looking birds.

> **Pocket fact**
>
> **Tiny raptor!**
> Microraptor gui, was one of the first raptor dinosaurs. It was less than two feet long and was covered in feathers.

> **Try this!**
>
> If you had to give some additional features to the Deinonychus, what would they be. Draw a picture to show these special features.

Why were Deinonychus's claws special?

Because of retracting talons! Deinonychus was a raptor with terrible claws—hence its name. It had three claws on its forelimbs and a large talon on its hind limbs. The dinosaur could retract the talons on its hind limbs, so that it could tuck them in for running and walking. Then it could bring them out again later to tear apart food.

Why didn't Sauropods walk on two legs?

Because they were heavy-weight! Sauropods were the largest animals to have ever lived on land. They were herbivores, and were usually quadrupeds, that is, they walked on four legs. They had small heads with large, massive bodies and long, counter-balancing tails. Due to their gigantic size, the Sauropods had thick legs to support their weight, with blunt, balanced feet that had five toes.

Pocket fact

First discovered!
The Corythosaurus was a plant-eating dinosaur and its fossil was first discovered in 1911 by Barnum Brown near Red Deer River located in Alberta, Canada.

Find out

How fast could Sauropods walk and run?

Why did the Corythosaurus wear a helmet?

Corythosaurus was a duck-billed dinosaur with a hollow, bony crest, shaped like a helmet on top of its long head. The dinosaur may have used it to make sounds, as a cooling device or for courtship displays. Corythosaurus' olfactory lobes, the part of the brain that senses smell, were located within the crest. So, it is likely that the crest must have been used as a sense-of-smell enhancer. Males had larger crests than females and juveniles.

Why is the Struthiomimus called an ostrich mimic?

The Struthiomimus was a light-weight member of the pre-historic dinosaur world. It was medium sized, light in build and had a long neck. It also had long rear limbs that appeared to be suitable for great speed and distance coverage, like that of an ostrich. It was similar to the ostrich in terms of its strength, its nimble nature and even its likely feathers. Hence, it was named the Struthiomimus.

Pocket fact

We are the noisiest!
The Parasaurolophus were probably the noisiest of all dinosaurs. It is assumed that they might have made a bellowing sound, like a giant trumpet!

Why did Parasaurolophus have a crest on its head?

The Parasaurolophus belonged to the Hadrosaurs group of dinosaurs that were known for their strange head ornaments. It had a long, narrow, backward-curving crest that grew out of the back of its skull. The crest had long distinct tubes. Scientists believe that the two hollow tubes inside the crest might have been used to make distinctive sounds, distinctive enough to have been identified individually, so that they could call and communicate with others in their herd.

Try this!

Can you name any three dinosaurs that were similar to an ostrich?

Why were some meat-eating dinosaurs called Raptors?

They were fast-moving dinosaurs similar to birds! Raptor fossils have been found all over the world, including China, the United States and Argentina. They were slim, clever and fast dinosaurs with their bodies covered in feathers. In addition to feathers, they had a special, long-toe claw which was used to hold onto and kill the prey. Raptors also had flexible forearms that they used for grabbing.

Pocket fact

The first raptor dinosaurs appeared over 120 million years ago. *Microraptor gui*, as its name implies, was a tiny dinosaur, less than two feet long. It was covered in feathers and is considered the most bird-like dinosaur.

Try this!

When did hadrosaurs live on Earth?

Why were some dinosaurs grouped as hadrosaurs?

They had many similar characteristics! 'Hadrosaurs' were plant-eating dinosaurs that mostly moved about on two legs, although the larger species probably walked on all fours. They were dinosaurs with a horny beak for picking-off plants and very effective teeth for chewing. Hadrosaurs had massive and inflexible tails, tough beaks and numerous cheek teeth. Their thick torsos gave them the name hadrosaurs which means bulky lizard.

Why is the Oviraptor also called the 'egg hunter'?

It was thought to hunt eggs! The Oviraptor was a meat-eating dinosaur from the late Cretaceous period. In 1922, James B. Shackleford discovered the fossil of a plant-eating dinosaur called Protoceratops. Later, in 1924, a technician named George Olsen discovered a nest of dinosaur eggs near the same place and it was assumed that the eggs belonged to the Protoceratops. However, the dinosaur fossil found near this nest belonged to an Oviraptor, which led to the assumption that the Oviraptor was trying to steal the Protoceratops' eggs. This is how the Oviraptor earned its name "egg hunter". However, years later it was found that the eggs belonged to the Oviraptor itself and the dinosaur was only trying to protect its own eggs.

Find out

The Ankylosaurus's skin was covered with Osteoderms. What are Osteoderms?

Pocket fact

We care!
Some dinosaurs looked after their babies until they were old enough to take care of themselves. One such dinosaur was the Maiasaura that fed its babies and protected them too.

Why was it difficult to attack the Ankylosaurs?

Because it was the largest of all armoured dinosaurs! The Ankylosaurus lived about 70–65 million years ago. It had thick bony plates all over its body. Its head was also covered with plates and spikes. It even had bony plates around its eyelids! The dinosaur also had a bony club at the end of its tail. Such heavy armour made it difficult for other dinosaurs to attack the Ankylosaurus.

Why didn't some dinosaurs chew their food?

Because they didn't have molars! Palaeontologists have discovered that huge plant-eating dinosaurs did not chew their food but just gulped it. These dinosaurs had a grinding organ called a gizzard, just like birds, alligators and seals do. They would swallow stones as big as softballs. When they swallowed food, the rocks helped to mash the food up, turning it into pulp.

Pocket fact

We have gizzards too!
The grinding organ called gizzard is also found in the digestive tract of some present-day animals, including crocodiles, alligators, earthworms and even birds.

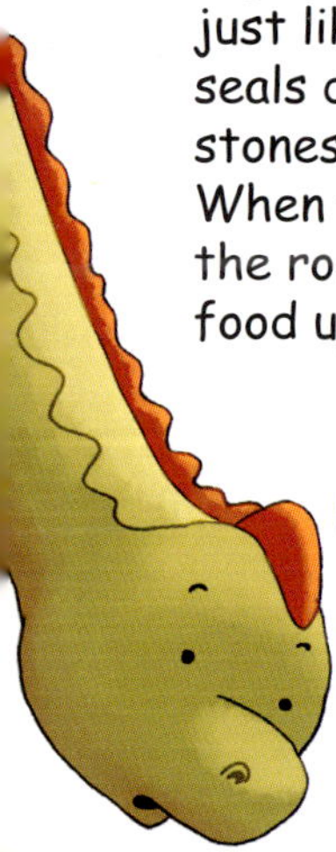

Find out

How big is a dinosaur tooth?

Why did the teeth of the Dilophosaurus break-off easily?

Because its jawbones were not strongly connected! The Dilophosaurus had several odd features, such as its jawbones were not strongly connected, it had a gap behind its forward teeth and its teeth also had a narrow base. This could have been the reason why its teeth might have broken-off more easily, while feeding, compared to the teeth of the other big meat eaters. Some scientists think that with all of these features, the Dilophosaurus could only have eaten fish or already dead animals.

Why did Euoplocephalus's eyes have bony shutters?

To protect itself from enemies! Euoplocephalus was a heavily-armoured dinosaur that lived in North America about 75 million years ago. It was covered with bony plates from head to tail. Its eyes were protected by armour. Each eyelid was actually a small, round bone that closed like a shutter when the dinosaur was attacked!

Pocket fact

What's my name!
Euoplocephalus was discovered by Lawrence Lambe in 1902. He proposed the name "Stereocephalus". However, the name "Stereocephalus" was already being used for an insect. Hence, the dinosaur was named Euoplocephalus in 1910.

Find out

Which dinosaur had a beak-shaped mouth without teeth?

Why did Sauropelta have both teeth and beak?

To gather low-growing plants and chew them! Sauropelta was an armoured dinosaur from the Cretaceous period. It looked a lot like the Ankylosaurus, but did not have a bony tail and horns on its head. Sauropelta had a narrow skull with big jaws and small, leaf-shaped cheek teeth. However, it did not have any front teeth but had a toothless horny beak. It used the beak to gather foliage and the small cheek teeth to mash them.

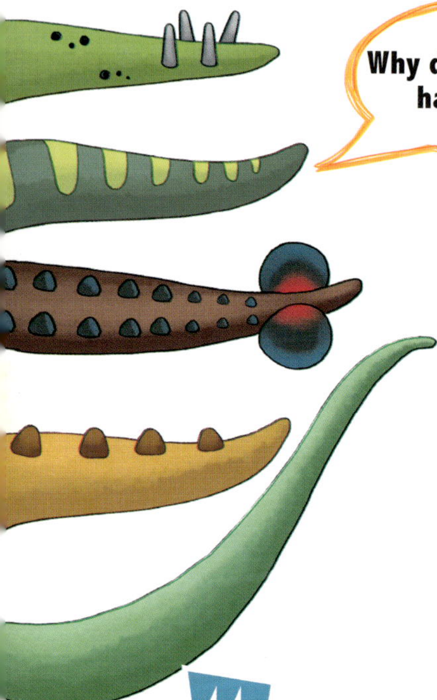

Why did dinosaurs have tails?

It served them several purposes! Most dinosaurs had large tails that had different uses. The tails of most dinosaurs helped them counterbalance their long neck or large, heavy head. The tails of fast-running dinosaurs helped them balance swift turns while running. Some dinosaurs like the Ankylosaurus had bony tails which they used for defense. And Sauropods had long whip-like tails that not only balanced their heavy body but also helped them scare away their enemies!

Find out

Which dinosaurs had holes in their jaws?

Pocket fact

That's the idea!
The idea that some Sauropods may have used their massive tails as a whip to lash at their attackers was given by the British zoologist R. McNeill Alexander in 1961.

Why did dinosaur skulls have windows?

To reduce the weight of the skull! Dinosaurs had holes in their skulls called "fenestrae," which means "windows" or "openings" in Latin. The ones located in the back portion of the skull were for the expansion of jaw muscles. The ones in front of the eye and sides were probably for lightening the skull, or for heat-loss purposes.

Why did T. Rex have small arms?

Because it didn't use them for hunting or walking! Most dinosaurs used their arms to walk or to hunt their prey. T. Rex, the king of dinosaurs, had small arms as compared to its body size. It was 42-feet long and weighed 7–9 tons. It walked on its hind limbs. It had a long tail that had over 40 bones, which helped balance the animals' huge head. It had 4-feet-long jaws filled with 50–60 sharp teeth. Its conical and serrated teeth were able to grab 500 pounds of meat in a single bite.

> **Pocket fact**
>
> **Extremely powerful!**
> Even though the T. Rex's arms were small as compared to its body but they were quite strong. It's believed that the T. Rex may have been capable of lifting approximately 450 pounds in each arm.

> **Try this!**
>
> Use an egg carton and a cupcake liner to make a model of the Triceratops. Use the carton for the face and the cupcake liner as a frill behind the Triceratops' head.

Why did the Triceratops wear a frill around its neck?

It had several functions! Triceratops was a large herbivore from the Late Cretaceous period. It had a big, bony frill extending from the back of its skull and covering its neck. The elaborate frill may have been used as armour to protect itself from its predators. The frill also had spikes that could have been used in the displays of rivals competing for territory or to attract mates.

Index

OTHER TITLES IN THIS SERIES

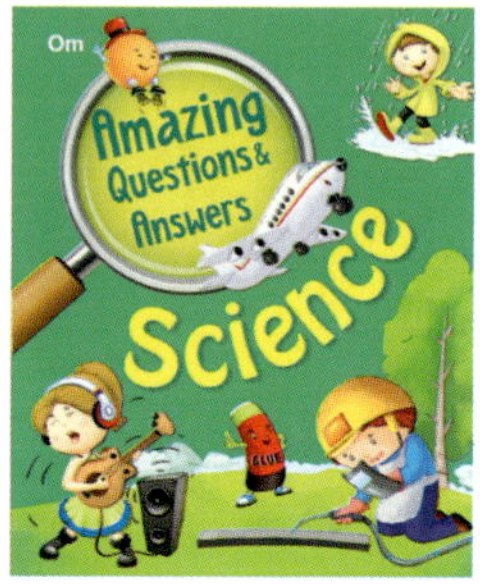

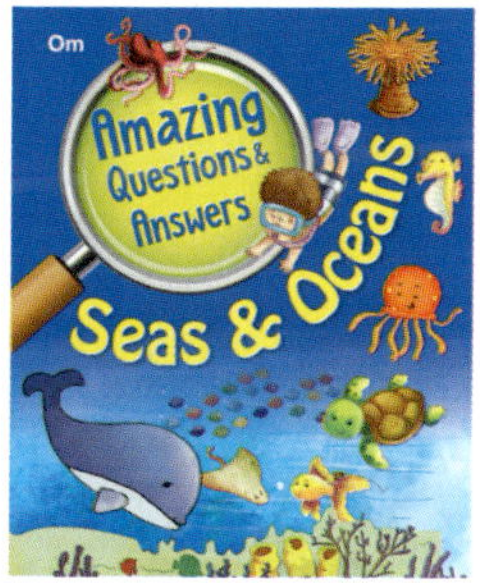